Pebble® Plus

Bugs, Bugs, Bugs!

Ladybugs

by Margaret Hall

Consulting Editor: Gail Saunders-Smith, PhD
Consultant: Gary A. Dunn, MS, Director of Education
Young Entomologists' Society Inc.
Lansing, Michigan

CAPSTONE PRESS
a capstone imprint
Mankato, Minnesota

Pebble Plus is published by Capstone Press,
1710 Roe Crest Drive, North Mankato, Minnesota 56003.
www.capstonepub.com

Library of Congress Cataloging-in-Publication Data
Hall, Margaret, 1947–
    Ladybugs/by Margaret Hall.
    p. cm.—(Pebble plus: Bugs, bugs, bugs!)
    Includes bibliographical references and index.
    ISBN-13: 978-0-7368-2589-4 (hardcover)
    ISBN-13: 978-0-7368-5097-1 (softcover pbk.)
    ISBN-13: 978-1-4296-5053-3 (saddle-stitch)
    1. Ladybugs—Juvenile literature. [1. Ladybugs.] I. Title. II. Series.
QL596.C65 H34 2005
595.76′9—dc22   2003024965

Summary: Simple text and photographs describe the physical characteristics and habits of ladybugs.

Editorial Credits
Sarah L. Schuette, editor; Linda Clavel, series designer; Kelly Garvin, photo researcher; Karen Hieb,
    product planning editor

Photo Credits
Bruce Coleman Inc./Gail M. Shumway, 6–7, 20–21; Kim Taylor, 12–13; Raymond Tercafs, 11
Digital Vision, 1
Robert & Linda Mitchell, cover, 5, 8–9, 15
Robert McCaw, 16-17
Stephen McDaniel, 18-19

Note to Parents and Teachers

The Bugs, Bugs, Bugs! series supports national science standards related to the diversity of life and heredity. This book describes and illustrates ladybugs. The images support early readers in understanding the text. The repetition of words and phrases helps early readers learn new words. This book also introduces early readers to subject-specific vocabulary words, which are defined in the Glossary section. Early readers may need assistance to read some words and to use the Table of Contents, Glossary, Read More, Internet Sites, and Index/Word List sections of the book.

Word Count: 98
Early-Intervention Level: 11

Printed in China.
092011   006411

Table of Contents

Ladybugs

What are ladybugs?

Ladybugs are insects

with spots.

5

How Ladybugs Look

Most ladybugs are red

or orange.

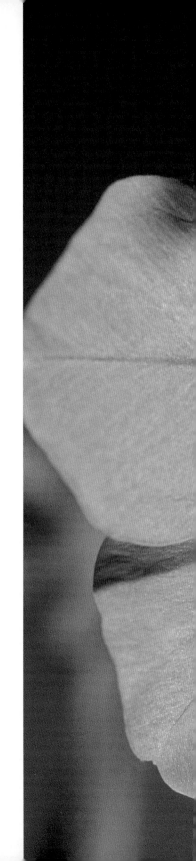

Ladybugs are about the size
of a small pea. Ladybugs
have six legs.

Ladybugs have two antennas. They touch and taste with their antennas.

Ladybugs have wings.
Thin wings help ladybugs
fly. Hard wings cover
the thin wings.

Ladybugs have sharp jaws.

They bite and chew with

their jaws.

What Ladybugs Do

Ladybugs sit in the sun. The sun keeps them warm.

Ladybugs lay eggs on plants. Young ladybugs hatch after a few weeks.

Ladybugs eat aphids.
One ladybug can eat
thousands of aphids
during its lifetime.

Glossary

antenna—a feeler; insects use antennas to sense movement, to smell, and to listen to each other.

aphid—a tiny insect that sucks and eats the juice out of plants

hatch—to break out of an egg

insect—a small animal with a hard outer shell, six legs, three body sections, and two antennas; most insects have wings.

Read More

Hughes, Monica. *Ladybugs.* Creepy Creatures. Chicago: Raintree, 2004.

Jango-Cohen, Judith. *Hungry Ladybugs.* Pull Ahead Books. Minneapolis: Lerner, 2003.

Posada, Mia. *Ladybugs: Red, Fiery, and Bright.* Minneapolis: Carolrhoda Books, 2002.

Internet Sites

FactHound offers a safe, fun way to find Internet sites related to this book. All of the sites on FactHound have been researched by our staff.

Here's how:

1. Visit *www.facthound.com*

2. Type in this special code **0736825894** for age-appropriate sites. Or enter a search word related to this book for a more general search.

3. Click on the **Fetch It** button.

FactHound will fetch the best sites for you!

Index/Word List